5 Essential Steps to
ORGANIZE
Your Home in 7 Days

A Realistic Approach to Organization

by

JANELLE R. WILLIAMS, MPH

Watersprings
PUBLISHING

5 Essential Steps to Organize Your Home In 7 Days:
A Realistic Approach to Organization
Published by Watersprings Publishing, a division of
Watersprings Media House, LLC.
P.O. Box 1284
Olive Branch, MS 38654
www.waterspringsmedia.com
Contact publisher for bulk orders and permission requests.

Printed in the United States of America.

Photos by Terrie Johnson Photography

ISBN-13: 978-1-948877-47-3

Table of Contents

To the loves of my life

To my husband, Darrell, this would not
be possible without your constant love, support,
and encouragement.

To my children, Jamari, Dakota, and Jude,
you inspire me every day to be the best version
of myself I can be.

To my parents, Kelly and Iolette Joseph,
thank you for your sacrifices and laying
the foundation for the woman I am today.

Acknowledgements

There are so many individuals in my life who have had an impact on me and have partnered with me as I've been on this journey of bringing this book to life. There are too many to name individually, but my gratitude towards each of you is abundant.

To my sister, brother, mother-in-law and family (immediate and extended), your support and words of encouragement have sustained and uplifted me over the past few years.

To my amazing sister friends I've been blessed with, I thank you for your listening ear and your unwavering friendship. There were times I may have wanted to give up, but you constantly reminded me of my why. Your late-night phone calls and text messages, outfit approvals, and numerous critiques have all played an intricate part in the fruition of this goal.

Finally, to my accountability partners and coach in business and life, I thank you! You all have been instrumental in not only bringing this business to life but in helping me shift my mindset around what is possible if you put in the work. I hope this book makes you proud!

Introduction

For many years, I was often asked how I kept my home so organized. To be quite honest, this was a somewhat difficult question for me to answer. You see, being organized came naturally for me. In fact, if you asked anyone who has known me personally, I've been this way from a very young age. As a child, I would constantly move things around our apartment and would also throw things away we did not use (my version of decluttering). Later on, during my college years, my roommates would always comment on how neat and organized my space was. Little did I know these would be the initial attributes of a budding Professional Organizer!

Growing up in a working-class family, I didn't have a lot of possessions and as a result, I was never a very materialistic person. I also didn't and still don't need, or like a ton of things in my space. Essentially, my life circumstances, in addition to some innate qualities, have enabled me to keep organized and focused on the things that are most important. Does this mean if you do not possess these qualities or had a similar background you can never get your home organized? No! In fact, even I have moments where things feel disorganized, but I have learned to put systems in place that will keep my home flowing almost seamlessly.

I know there are some of us who struggle with keeping our homes and essentially our lives in order. We tend to become so caught up in the day to day busyness of life that we allow things to build up to the point where we become overwhelmed. However, there is always hope! True organization necessitates a shift in your mindset. It requires consistency, discipline, and determination.

With this approach, it is possible for anyone to learn and implement the steps needed to simplify your home and life. So, if you're ready to take the first step, let's walk through the five essential steps to prioritize and organize your home in seven days.

"Your physical clutter affects your mental state..."

– JANELLE WILLIAMS MPH

CHAPTER ONE

Shift Your Mindset

When we delve into the task of getting organized, we tend to overlook the importance of our "mindset" in this process. There has been an enormous amount of research done on mindset and the effect it has on our behavior. According to psychologist Dr. Gary Klein in *Psychology Today*, a mindset is "a belief that orients the way we handle situations; it is the way we sort out what is going on and what we should do" (Klein, 16). The fact is when we are accustomed to doing things a specific way it inevitably becomes a habit. In order to change that behavior, we must adjust our way of thinking. Subsequently, to break that mindset, we must first identify why we believe what we believe.

Once you have identified the "why" then you are able to put simple systems in place that will allow you to address the behavior. For example, if you consistently allow your mail to accumulate until it gets to the point that it becomes overwhelming, then you need to first understand the why. Why am I doing this and what am I doing or not doing that accommodates this behavior?

Once you have identified your why, the next step is to put a process in place that would prevent this from occurring. For some of us, it requires that we change our thought process of "I will get to this later when I have the time," and instead setting aside a scheduled time to get the task done (known as time blocking). Or it could even include something as simple as setting an alarm on your phone as a weekly reminder.

Implementing a system for you to regularly achieve this task will enable you to become more efficient and not become overwhelmed. In this instance you have sorted out your why, your thought process, and then created a system to address the behavior. You will also find that time can often be an obstacle in this process, however you must mentally train yourself to prioritize and make the time to get your home in order. Consider it an investment now that will pay off in time saved later.

One of the biggest obstacles to getting organized is not being able to let go of your possessions. The inability to rid yourself of unnecessary things also has a lot to do with your mindset. Have you ever heard the saying, "collect moments and not things"? It's a reminder for us to cherish life's experiences and not our belongings. We tend to hold on to things for a number of reasons that don't necessarily make sense. Whether we are holding on to clothing for 10 years because we are losing the weight to fit back into them, or hoarding all of our college papers sitting in a box collecting dust.

It is important to realize that this will hinder your ability to put systems in place that will allow your homes (and your lives) to run more efficiently.

I make it a habit to be mindful about the perceived value of things I own daily. The things will fade away; therefore, if the things that I am holding on to are simply not useful anymore, it is okay to let them go. Getting rid of the unnecessary stuff in our homes is one of the first steps to an organized lifestyle, however you must shift your thought process (mindset) away from the accumulation of things.

Let's think in practical terms. If you have had an item for an extended period of time and year after year it continues to occupy your space without being used, do you honestly believe that you *need* it? Chances are you may just have an issue with letting go and need to address your attachment to that item.

Ultimately, you can read all the blogs and books that give you tips to be more organized, and you can even hire a professional organizer to do the work for you. However, if you have not addressed your way of thinking and subsequently your habits, you will more than likely end up in the same predicament. Before you embark on this journey, I encourage you to take the time to explore your mindset and how it affects your ability to truly live a more simplified life.

Action Item

Below are some questions to consider as you explore
your mindset with regards to organization.

What am I doing that accommodates certain habits?

_____

_____

_____

_____

*Is it that I really don't have the time, or do I need to make the
time to complete certain tasks?*

_____

_____

_____

_____

_____

Do I have an emotional attachment to this item? Why?

_____

_____

_____

_____

Does the" stuff" give me an emotional high?

_____

_____

_____

_____

_____

_____

_____

_____

_____

_____

_____

**"For every minute spent
in organizing an hour
is earned..."**

– BENJAMIN FRANKLIN

CHAPTER TWO

Create Schedules

In 2007, we purchased our first home. After 5 years of being a stay at home mom, I went back to work full-time. To top it off, we moved from one state to another, and my husband stayed behind because he had not found a full-time position in our new home state. I was in a new state with two young children working full-time and by myself. In order for me to run my home efficiently, I quickly realized I needed to implement techniques that would simplify tasks. One of the first things I did was create a schedule for myself and our two little ones in order to create some structure for our home.

Just as adults need structure in their work life and children have structure at school or daycare, that same approach should apply in the home. Establishing specific time frames for when things are done on a daily, weekly and monthly basis, as well as being consistent goes a long way to creating a structured environment. This not only applies to homes with children but to those without children. Schedules help us establish better routines, which ultimately lead to more structured environments.

We have established the need to adjust our mindset to get our homes in order; now let's explore some practical steps to achieve this.

Since organization focuses on prioritizing and increasing productivity, creating schedules is a crucial step in the process. In our home, we have created a few different schedules to assist with keeping our home organized. We have a schedule for our daily activities such as eating dinner, completing homework, making the bed and other day to day tasks. Again, we used time-blocking to specify the time frame for each activity, in the evenings from 4-9 PM and in the mornings from 7-9 AM.

Our weekly schedule consists of the days when specific tasks or chores are done. For example, although we are a family of 5, we do not do laundry every day. The goal is to do a load every few days (once or twice a week), which saves not only time but money. For other household chores, we try to do a little every day. However, since our day to day schedules can be very busy at times, we do more time-consuming chores on a once per week basis (usually on a Friday afternoon after school/work).

The sole purpose of utilizing a schedule is to be as consistent as possible so that you do not become overwhelmed with tackling too many tasks at once. Over time, as you incorporate schedules into your home you will recognize what works best for you or your family.

As you are creating schedules, you will find that some things require different time frames and may not need to be tackled weekly or even monthly. For example, I encourage my clients to declutter their homes quarterly, so this would be included on a yearly calendar or schedule. However, if you are in the initial stages of getting your home organized you may find that you need to declutter more often. Taking inventory of your clothing and other items in the home is just as important as your daily responsibilities because it helps you to prioritize and get rid of unnecessary items.

After you have tackled creating the schedule(s), it's now time to implement. I'm sure you've heard this a million times, but I would suggest actually making a poster of your schedule(s) and placing it where the entire household (or just you if you're a household of one) can see, especially if this is the beginning of your journey to simplifying your home life. Then, be as consistent as possible with following that schedule until it becomes the norm. Research shows that once your mind is trained to do something on a consistent basis, it becomes second nature to you.

So, take some time before you begin the next step to establish the schedule(s) for your household. Think about the areas where you may need more structure and where you need to manage your time more efficiently. Think about your timeframes such as doing things on a daily, weekly, monthly or yearly basis. WRITE IT DOWN and IMPLEMENT!!!

Action Item

Since we are working on 7 days to an organized home let's create a schedule and outline what aspects or areas of your home you would like to tackle. Grab a calendar and pick 7 days where you can allocate at least 6 hours per day to the process. They don't have to be 7 consecutive days; however, I'd suggest not having too long of a lapse in between each day to sustain the momentum. Use the graph below to help you create a 7-day plan for your home.

7 Day Schedule

	Day 1	Day 2	Day 3	Day 4	Day 5	Day 6	Day 7
Choose 1 Area							
Step 1							
Step 2							
Step 3							
Step 4							
Step 5							

❝It is better to take many small steps in the right direction than to make a great leap forward only to stumble backward...❞

– OLD CHINESE PROVERB

CHAPTER THREE

Start Small

You can't organize your entire home (or even a room) in one day; it is a process. To be successful, you should start with one space or area. It could be a kitchen cabinet or a dresser drawer. If you are ambitious, it could be a small pantry or closet. Starting with one small area and using simple methods will ensure success by giving you the motivation needed to tackle the bigger jobs.

If you were to take a survey of individuals who consider themselves to be organized, they would probably tell you that their journey was filled with much trial and error. The road to getting organized did not transpire overnight; it was a process. Therefore, you don't want to overwhelm yourself with attempting a huge space initially.

Here is a real-life example of why starting small is important from a client. As a psychiatrist and consultant, my client has treated numerous patients with mental health issues including hoarding, but she realized her family also struggled with the tendency to accumulate clutter. Her family of four had accumulated a massive amount of clothing that had completely taken over their home. It became such a nuisance that even putting away their clothes after laundry day seemed like an impossible task. Fed up, they decided it was time to do something. A family member decided to bring ALL their clothing from every inch of their home into the family room so they could essentially declutter and organize all their clothing.

Instead of "starting small" they decided to tackle all their clothing at once. Let's just say it was days before they were able to go through all their clothes and several weeks before their family room was fully functional again because the process became too overwhelming for them. I eventually came in and helped them through the process by tackling one closet and one bedroom at a time.

Starting small is also important when it comes to decluttering because this process can be extremely draining both physically and mentally. Purging and sorting through items, deciding what to discard and what to keep for hours at a time is demanding. That's why most professional organizers work as a team and in blocks of time. Not only should you start with a smaller space, but you should also pace yourself by working in 4-6-hour blocks of time and then take a break.

Often times, when we try to tackle too much at once we become frustrated and are discouraged from continuing what we set out to accomplish in the first place. This in turn has an adverse effect on not only the state of our physical space, but our mental state as well. This is another reason why it is so important to start small.

Make a list of the problem areas in your home and number them from 1 to 10 with 10 being the most difficult area. Then I'd like you to start with the area that needs the least amount of work. For example, if the most difficult place in your home to keep organized is your pantry, don't start there. Start with one of your kitchen cabinets or a drawer. After you have tackled a few of your cabinets, then you can move on to the pantry. The pantry is usually a bit more time consuming and will require a little more patience. Once you see the transformation of a smaller area and you understand the process, it will be much easier to tackle a larger space.

Action Item

Home Project Worksheet

List problem areas of your home from 1 to 10
(10 being the most difficult):

1. _____

2. _____

3. _____

4. _____

5. _____

6. _____

7. _____

8. _____

9. _____

10. _____

Choose one small area to tackle, such as one kitchen cabinet at a time. Then move on to the next cabinet and work your way up to the pantry.

"If it doesn't matter, get rid of it..."

– BANKSY

CHAPTER FOUR

Declutter And Take Inventory

When you have a family or you are a busy professional, keeping your home organized can be extremely challenging. From the clothes to the shoes and the toys, it can all become overwhelming if you are not diligent about maintaining all of the "stuff." According to a recent article in the New York Times Professor of Psychology at DePaul University, Joseph Ferrari, states, "Clutter is an overabundance of possessions that collectively create chaotic and disorderly living spaces." This supports research that indicates when we are surrounded by clutter, we become overwhelmed and anxious (Murphy, 17).

Subsequently, this hinders our ability to complete tasks in our homes and at work. Therefore scheduling "inventory" (decluttering) is important. You should consistently be going through your possessions a few times a year and getting rid of items that don't serve a purpose anymore. This is one of the most important steps of the organization process. So how do we start the process of decluttering? The first step to decluttering is to remove every item from the space. It's important to clear out the space completely because often you will find items that are damaged, soiled or items you did not even realize you had. It also enables you to examine each item individually and make intentional decisions. Lastly, removing everything creates a clean slate to work with and makes it easier for you to create a streamlined system.

Next, we need to go through the items and sort them *(this is an initial sort, you'll do a more detailed sort in the next step)*. To make the sorting process easier, it is recommended that you create 3 piles; KEEP, DONATE, and DISCARD. Keep this simple! Too many piles will overwhelm you. If you prefer you can use a bin, garbage bag, or box to sort your items. However, you can also use any open floor or table space to sort your piles.

KEEP

Keep only the things you know will be used. It is important to be very intentional about what is placed in this pile as these will be the items that remain in your edited space. If you are unsure about whether to keep a specific item, that's a good indication that you may not really want or need it. You also want to be careful about keeping items for "just in case." Those items tend to be the source for most of the clutter in our homes.

DONATE

Donate only items that are still in decent condition. Your donation pile can consist of things you plan to donate or sell as well. These are usually things that are still useful, but they have served their purpose for your home, and you no longer need them. Be intentional about what goes into this pile as well; it's not the pile for junk. Once you've done an initial sort, you will then want to separate your donation pile into what to donate or sell. When you are thinking about selling an item, make sure it is something that you would purchase at a second-hand store or yard sale. If an item has any damage, it's best to discard it.

DISCARD

Discard any items that are expired, chipped, cracked, or torn. I have found that many people confuse what you should donate and what you should discard, especially when it comes to clothing. Even if you are donating an item to organizations such as Goodwill, you want to ensure it is still usable. Anything that's not, you should discard. You'll also want to check with donation centers for a list of items that they don't accept, so you can discard those items beforehand.

Let's look at an example of how we would declutter our toiletries. The first step in decluttering the toiletries, would be to gather and remove all of them from the space. After we have removed everything, we need to

examine all items to see what items are used regularly or items that are backstock (**KEEP**), or used occasionally (**DONATE**), and what is empty or expired (**DISCARD**). Once we've eliminated items that are empty or expired then the remaining items can be sorted into categories. If you have toiletries that are used occasionally, or not used at all, you may be able to donate them to a local shelter if the items are in good condition.

When we take the time to examine our habits, we'll find that we usually use the same personal care items daily. Therefore, it is imperative we are taking inventory and decluttering these items regularly. The process of decluttering is not necessarily for you to get rid of ALL your things but for you to be more intentional about the things in your home. Let's look at some of the major categories where routine inventory is vital.

CLOTHING INVENTORY: Just as the seasons change, our personal style also changes. Be sure to thoroughly examine your clothing and accessories after every season. Eliminate items you haven't used within 12-18 months. Start with the obvious, which are items that don't fit or are damaged. Then, discard items that don't reflect your personal style anymore. For some individuals, their fluctuation in weight can be a hinderance to discarding clothing. In fact, according to a study by Elizabeth Bye and Ellen McKinney, they found that most of the individuals they evaluated kept specific articles of clothing with the expectation that their weight would alter and were reluctant to discard those items (Bye & McKinney, 07). So, if you are working on a weight loss goal, you may keep a few items for your

ideal weight. However, those items should not occupy your "primary" clothing area.

TOY INVENTORY: Children's toys (and some adult toys too) can lead to a vast amount of clutter and disorder in the home. In fact, many families oftern become overwhelmed by the magnitude of items. Instead of addressing the problem, they continue to buy "bins" to conceal things instead of resolving the problem. While I am a huge advocate of using storage pieces to aid in containing items, the main concern is to limit the amount of unnecessary clutter in the space. Decluttering will help to limit the clutter and keep your children's toys organized.

If you're not using the something in, something out rule you will only continue to add to the clutter.

It's always a good idea to schedule regular inventory of your children's toys. Every few months, check to see what toys your child doesn't really play with. If they are in good condition, donate them. If they are not in the best of condition or don't work, discard them. Create a schedule for routine inventory; I'd suggest every quarter or every season and stick to it.

DIGITAL INVENTORY: From our pictures, to our emails, to our downloads and social sites, our digital clutter is another huge category where routine inventory is necessary. Digital clutter is also one of the major sources of mental clutter, so it is imperative that we "schedule" time to go through these items and edit regularly, especially if this is an area you struggle with maintaining. For downloads on your phone or computer, to lessen the visual clutter, you can create folders and categorize documents or apps.

The same concept of creating folders can also be applied to your emails in addition to making sure you are blocking time to go through those emails on a weekly basis. Schedule a seasonal inventory of your pictures. After every season, take some time to upload pictures from your phone to your computer or create a photo book. Associating the task with a season makes it more manageable and easier to categorize.

PAPER INVENTORY: Routine inventory of your household documents and any papers that enter your home is crucial in keeping your home in order. To stay ahead of the paper clutter, you must tackle it immediately. However, if you're not the most disciplined with decluttering your papers, time-blocking is essential to accomplish this task. This correlates to Chapter 2 where we discussed creating schedules for specific tasks. Before you tackle your paper clutter, you'll need to establish two major groupings: one for long-term document storage and the other for your immediate action storage.

Next, you'll want to have an inbox for incoming mail or papers, then a recycling and shred bin. Recycle any unwanted papers and shred anything that contains sensitive information *(if you do not already have one, invest in a shredder).*

If you find that you're constantly getting junk mail from the same company, don't be afraid to call and ask to be removed from their list. Implementing these simple methods will aid in minimizing the clutter from the papers that enter your space.

"A place for everything and everything in its place..."

– BENJAMIN FRANKLIN

CHAPTER FIVE

Let's Get Organized

Now that you have decluttered and taken inventory, we can move on to the final phase of organizing your home. In order to be truly successful with getting organized it is essential that you go through this entire process. From shifting your mindset to the physical act of decluttering your space, each step is vital for success. In this step we will explore how to establish sustainable systems to help restore order in your home.

A PLACE FOR EVERYTHING: Having a designated place for your items keeps clutter to a minimum and keeps your space in order. The first step in the organizing phase is to identify a specific place for specific items. This may seem rudimentary, but what I've experienced with clients is that there are usually items in areas of the home where they probably shouldn't be. For example, many people have papers in several areas of their home, including their master or main bedroom. They never really established an area of the home where their papers should "reside". This is where issues arise when you are trying to locate your belongings because there was never a designated space for where papers would be stored. Does this sound familiar? To resolve this, we need to establish one main area in your home to tackle and store your papers. Hence the phrase, "a place for everything and everything in its place!" Designating a specific place for specific items essentially assigns a location for your belongings so that you can locate them easily. You will also find this helps significantly with maintenance and returning items to where they belong.

CATEGORIES MATTER: Once we've established a place where our items will reside, the next step is to categorize. This is where you will put like items together. Again, although this may seem minimal, it is a

vital part of creating order. When you are choosing your categories, you don't want to be too specific or too broad, and you also want to make sure that the categories you choose will be easy for everyone in your home to maintain.

Let's look at an example in the pantry. Perhaps you have several types of pasta or rice products. Instead of separating each product in a different container, use one container where all the rice or pasta products could be stored. This also helps to save space if you have limited space. If you have the space and can consistently decant then by all means you can use different containers for each food type. However, if this creates any added hassle for you, then stick to using one bin.

Here is another practical example of how to compartmentalize your belongings. Instead of arbitrarily putting clothes in your drawer with no system in place, try placing them in categories. For example, place all your "outdoor" wear in one drawer and all "sleeping/ play" wear in another drawer. Or you can get even more specific with the type of item like placing all sweatshirts and all sweatpants in a drawer or bin. Placing your things into categories allows you to see exactly how much of an item you have and helps reduce the number of multiples.

CONTAINMENT: Now that you have sorted and categorized your items the next step is to contain those items. I cannot stress enough how important it is to sort through your items before you purchase anything to contain them. I've coined this "assess before you acquire!" When working with clients, I'll often request that they send me pictures of their spaces or do an initial walk through so that I can do an assessment of what they have first before we purchase any containers. Doing this beforehand allows you to choose the appropriate size and type of containment you'll need for your space.

So how do we know what containers to purchase? First, you'll need to measure the designated area where you plan to store your items. For instance, if you are working on a closet project and you want to add bins to the existing shelving, you'll need to measure the height, depth and length of your shelves so you can choose the appropriate size and number of bins. Next, think about what you'll be storing in the containers. Is it toiletries, food items or clothing? This is important to keep in mind when choosing the type of containment.

It's important not to only focus on the aesthetics, but also the functionality. For example, for food items such as onions or potatoes stored in the pantry, you may not want to use baskets that are made of woven material or cloth. Those items can be messy, and you'll want to clean the containers occasionally so choose a material that will be easy to clean like acrylic or BPA free plastic bins. The same can be said for certain toiletry items as well. Choose a material that will hold up to the stains and spills that one can expect. Finally, consider your personal style. You'll want to choose containment that suits your existing space and creates a cohesive look, but also have fun and add pops of color to reflect your personality!

CREATE A STREAMLINED LOOK: Once you've contained your items, using labels helps to easily identify where to place your items. For me "labels are the icing on the cake", you may not necessarily need them however they help create a streamlined appearance. If you're an organizing fanatic, then the type of labels can become extremely complex. However, I like to opt for keeping things simple.

Most of the labels I use for clients are handwritten, but I often use a simple label maker (*DYMO Handheld Label Maker*) that you can find at any office supply store. Now for those who may want a more polished look without the need for expensive or complicated gadgets, here's my secret.

I use the **AVERY 22822 glossy clear labels** with a desktop printer *(see picture below),* which gives the look of vinyl labels but for less! Allow the labels to dry for at least one hour before applying or for speed use a blow dryer. No matter how you create your labels, they are a key component in keeping a space organized.

CREATE ZONES: Lastly, creating zones helps keep our "necessary" clutter contained in specific areas. The specific zones may be unique for every home or family, but these are the TOP 3 zones I've found that are necessary in every home to keep things organized and running efficiently.

1. Command Center Zone

The command center is a central area that is the hub of your home, like an information center. This is a space or area that you keep a calendar, activities schedule, mail, and most importantly your KEYS. Having a central area in your home where everyone can see what is scheduled and can access things easily is helpful in keeping you and/or your family on track.

2. Drop Zone

A drop zone is an area designated to keep jackets, shoes, bags and sports equipment. It eliminates the clutter and confusion that often occurs during the hectic morning and afternoon routines. The key to creating a functional drop zone is placement, having this strategically placed in an area where your family enters/exits your home is important.

3. Lunch/Snack Zone (Pantry & Refrigerator)

Finally, a lunch/snack zone in your pantry and refrigerator minimizes the chaos of hectic mornings. Fridge Prep is all the rage now and is extremely helpful when planning for the work/school week. Kids can access what they need by themselves without creating a mess, and it also helps you to plan better when it comes to grocery shopping. Prep baggies of fruits and veggies and store them in containers in your refrigerator and keep non-perishable snack items in a labeled bin in your pantry.

While there is no one size fits all with organizing a space, these methods will equip you with the tools and knowledge necessary to create sustainable systems for your home. We all deserve to have a space that is well ordered and functions efficiently.

Create a drop zone to eliminate clutter at the entrance of your home.

Action Item

We've covered a few methods within the organization step so let's recap them again and write down our ideas:

1. Have a designated place for your items. Where should you keep certain items in your home? (Write them down here)

   _____

   _____

   _____

   _____

   _____

   _____

2. Sort and categorize by putting like with like items. (Write down your categories as you are sorting, this will help you with your labels later)

   _____

   _____

   _____

   _____

   _____

   _____

3. Contain your items. (If you are purchasing bins, write down how many bins you'll need per category here)

_____

_____

_____

_____

_____

4. Create a streamlined look. (Here is where you can make a list of your labels after you've identified the categories)

_____

_____

_____

_____

_____

_____

5. Create Zones. (Think about what zones your home needs to make it run more efficiently)

_____

_____

_____

_____

_____

❝Organization is more than just a pretty picture; it's about managing life efficiently.❞

– JANELLE WILLIAMS MPH

Conclusion

There are many benefits to having a space that is clutter free and organized. You are better prepared for any emergencies that may arise. You have the ability to locate and identify your items easily, as well as peace of mind and decreased stress. It's much more than just crafting a beautiful after picture; it's restoring order to the chaos that clutters your minds and your spaces. This is why, it's imperative that you make the time to declutter and get organized despite the busyness of life.

As you begin the journey to reclaiming your space, here are a few things to keep in mind. First, keep it simple! The systems you put in place don't have to be elaborate or extravagant to be effective. Maybe that means you may not have the label with the perfectly curated font or impeccable built-in shelving. But if you can locate your items more effortlessly now with just a simple handwritten label, then you've successfully accomplished the goal.

Second, don't break the bank! The huge misconception is that you need to spend an enormous amount of money on products in order to get your space organized. I encourage you to do your research before you purchase any products and consider the option that makes the most sense for your time and budget. Also take advantage of sales that many stores have on containers several times during the year, specifically in January and the Spring. You can always schedule your projects during those months.

Finally, consider reaching out for help. Sometimes, due to the emotional ties we may have with our belongings it can be hard to let go. Or maybe the task seems too overwhelming for you to handle it alone. Having an outside person who can be objective may be what you need to help you make intentional and thoughtful choices.

Now that you have successfully navigated the 5 essential steps of getting your home in order; it's time to take the leap. Let's double back and look at the 10 areas you listed on your home project worksheet and tackle each area from 1 to 10, using the 5 steps outlined for you. Finalize your 7-day plan to tackle each space individually (there will be some areas where more than one can be completed in a day) and remember to start with your least difficult areas and then tackle the larger projects.

I hope this book has supported you by giving you a guide from which to not only get organized, but to make better choices in terms of what you allow to dwell in your home. Be deliberate with your purchases so that you are not unnecessarily buying items you already have in excess. The task of getting your home organized may seem overwhelming at the outset, but it is not impossible. When you put systems in place for your home and life, it truly allows you to be free to do the things you love to do!

De-clutter Checklist

☐ *If you haven't used an item in a year, even though you think you may need it, get rid of it.*

☐ *Donate, donate, donate! If you don't want to throw an item away because it's still in good condition, donate it. Also, donate items on a schedule, every 3 months or quarterly.*

☐ *If you have multiple items that are similar or that you use for the same purpose, then get rid of one or a few.*

☐ *Use all possible storage areas. Take advantage of every nook in your home to store your necessary items.*

☐ *Create a budget to cut spending. If you tend to buy things you don't necessarily need, having a budget will deter you from spending money on unnecessary items.*

☐ *Instead of buying something new, reuse or repurpose an item you already have.*

Household Checklist

Morning & Night

- ☐ *Make my bed & devotion*
- ☐ *Brush my teeth & wash my face*
- ☐ *Lotion my skin & brush my hair*
- ☐ *Hang up my sleeping clothes*
- ☐ *Afternoon snack and free time*
- ☐ *Do homework*
- ☐ *Take a bath, and bedtime at 8 PM!*

My room is clean when...

- ☐ *My bed is made*
- ☐ *My toys are in their bins*
- ☐ *There is nothing on the floor*
- ☐ *My clean clothes are put away*
- ☐ *My dirty clothes are in the hamper*

The kitchen is clean when...

- ☐ *The floor is swept*
- ☐ *The trash and recycling are empty*
- ☐ *The clean dishes are put away*
- ☐ *There are no dishes in the sink*
- ☐ *The tables and counters are clean; food is put away*

Household Document Checklist

Documents to keep indefinitely

- ☐ *Legal documents (birth certificates, marriage license, divorce papers, passports)*
- ☐ *Pension plan records, Retirement plan records & Wills*
- ☐ *Receipts for major purchases (for warranty and insurance purposes)*
- ☐ *Deeds, mortgages and bills of sale*
- ☐ *Year-end statements for investments*
- ☐ *Education records (transcript, diploma)*
- ☐ *Current insurance policies*
- ☐ *Automobile titles*
- ☐ *Annual tax returns (last 7 years)*

Documents to keep up to 7 years

- ☐ *Annual tax returns*
- ☐ *W-2 and 1099 forms*
- ☐ *Receipts for tax purposes*
- ☐ *Medical bills or claims for tax purposes*
- ☐ *Disability records & unemployment stubs*
- ☐ *Bank statements (electronically)*

Documents to trash or recycle

- ☐ *Store receipts (groceries, clothing, accessories)*
- ☐ *Old magazines or newspapers*
- ☐ *Coupons after expiration date*
- ☐ *Expired warranties*
- ☐ *Paycheck stubs after reconciling with W-2 form*
- ☐ *College coursework (unless used for reference material)*

Note: If you are starting a huge decluttering project of papers, I would suggest using a shredding company to help with that process. Check out the resources section for more information on shredding companies.

Resources

Book Donations

www.discoverbooks.com (mission is to divert books from landfills and help fund library sustainability)

www.readertoreader.org (online source that provides free, used books to under-resourced schools and public libraries)

www.betterworldbooks.com (donated books are sold online to help raise funds for non-profit literacy organizations)

Online Clothing & Furniture Donations

www.pickupplease.org (online source for donating gently used household goods, clothing, toys, electronics, and small furniture)

www.gogreendrop.com (online source for donating clothing, bedding, electronics, and small appliances)

www.donationtown.org (online source for donating clothing and other household goods to charity)

Antique & Estate Sale

www.foursales.com (online estate sale)

www.maxsold.com (online estate sale firm)

Shredding Companies (online & local)

www.theupsstore.com UPS Stores

www.shredit.com (online document destruction services)

www.amsstoreandshred.com (national document destruction service)

Appendix

Le Beau Lucchesi, Emilie. (2019). *The Unbearable Heaviness of Clutter.* Section D, Page 4. New York: The New York Times.

Klein Ph.D., Gary. (2016). Mindsets, what they are and why they matter. *Psychology Today.* Sussex Publishers.

Murphy, Heather. (2017). *What We Finally Got Around to Learning at the Procrastination Research Conference.* New York. The New York Times.

Bye, Elizabeth; McKinney, Ellen. (2007). Sizing Up the Wardrobe, Why We Keep Clothes That Do Not Fit. *Fashion Theory. Volume 11, Issue 4.* Fashion Theory.

About The Author

As a busy mom of three, wife, and entrepreneur, Janelle had to develop systems that would help her prioritize and manage the stress of home, work, and life.

She has always had a passion for working with people. After years of assisting family and friends with transforming their homes into efficient and functional spaces, she decided to pursue her business full-time. Her passion is to assist clients with understanding the "why" behind the clutter and creating personalized systems that enable them to improve efficiency and quality of life.

Janelle holds a Master's in Public Health. After working with government and non-profit organizations for several years, she started her consulting business in 2016. As the Owner and Lead Professional Organizer she assists families, small businesses, and professionals to create systems that help them de-clutter, simplify and increase efficiency.

To find out more information about Janelle or work with her, follow the links below:

Website:
janellewilliamsconsulting.com
http://janellewilliamsconsulting.com/

Facebook:
Janelle Williams Professional Organizer
https://www.facebook.com/organizedbyjwc/

Instagram:
Organized by JWC
https://www.instagram.com/organizedbyjwc/

Pinterest:
Organized by JWC
https://www.pinterest.com/Organizedbyjwc/